Lone Wolf

Susan Gates
Illustrated by Geoff Taylor

OXFORD

Chapter 1 – Shot!

"Stay right where you are, you little pest!" murmured the hunter. He was hiding in the forest, watching the wolf cub.

"What's it doing on its own?" he wondered. Wolf families usually guard their cubs carefully. They fight to the death to defend them.

"Must have got lost," thought the hunter. It was a pity the cub wasn't full grown yet. Still, a little one was better than nothing.

He took aim.

Grey, the wolf cub, spotted the hunter moving. But it was too late.

Zing!

The bullet cracked off a rock next to Grey's head and scraped along his side. Yelping with pain, he scurried into some bramble bushes. He burrowed in as deep as he could, not caring how much the thorns scratched him. He lay in the centre, panting and whimpering, licking his wound.

In the wilderness where the wolves lived, Grey had never seen a human before. But he'd just learned one valuable lesson: avoid them.

This particular human wasn't going to give up easily. He was a patient man and he wanted a wolf skin to hang on his wall.

He sat, very quietly, watching the bramble bushes and waiting.

Chapter 2 – Danger!

It had started out as such a good day. That morning, Grey had set off with his family on his first hunting trip.

The family trotted in single file through the forest. Grey's mum and dad, the pack leaders, were at the front. His grandma, aunts and uncles, older brothers and sisters, followed behind. Last in line came Grey and the other three youngest cubs.

Grey stopped for a quick play fight with his sister. They pounced on each other, wrestling and rolling over and over.

"Yip, yip, yip!" Grey yelped as his sister nipped his ear and ran off. Grey chased her, skidding like a skater, using his big wolf feet as brakes.

A warning bark came from one of the adult wolves. It meant, "Stop messing about back there!"

Grey didn't obey fast enough – he gave his sister a last swipe with his paw.

"Yow!" Grey protested as Grandma snapped at him, snarling and showing her teeth. Her snarls meant, "Keep quiet!" Catching food was serious business. A noisy wolf cub could spoil the whole hunt.

Grandma made the cubs behave, but she played with them too. She gave them scraps of fur to pounce on and bite. She chased them with deer antlers in her mouth. If they were too slow, they got a sharp poke.

The cubs didn't know yet that these weren't just games. Grandma was teaching them important lessons that would help them defend themselves against danger.

Whimpering, Grey slunk back to his place in the line.

The four cubs had been born in late spring in a den, deep among tree roots. At first, they had been blind and deaf, helpless as kittens. But after only four weeks, they had climbed out of the den. They started exploring everything, sniffing and biting with their small prickly teeth.

Their mum had then gone off hunting with the rest of the pack, but the four cubs were never left alone. Someone always stayed behind to defend them. Sometimes it was their dad or grandma, sometimes an older brother or aunt. Everyone in the family took turns to look after the cubs.

Now the cubs were three months old. They weren't cute little fuzzballs any more. They were lean, young wolves, with teeth that could crunch bones and tear flesh, and long legs that could run fast.

Just not quite fast enough to keep up with the pack. They weren't fully grown yet. They still had a lot to learn.

The family ran on, tails wagging eagerly. The adults stopped now and then to scent mark. That was a warning to other wolf packs: "Stay away! This is our territory!"

"Grrrr!"

The whole family stopped. That growl from the cubs' dad meant, "Wait! There's danger."

Chapter 3 – Swept away!

The way was blocked by a river. The wolves weren't usually scared of water. They were good swimmers. But this river was fast-flowing, with whirlpools and waterfalls. It would have to be crossed with care. Grey's dad scouted up and down the bank. He yipped in excitement. He had found the place where the deer had crossed. If deer could cross safely here, it should be no problem for wolves.

He scrambled down the bank, slid into the water and began paddling towards the far bank. His family followed him.

It should have been safe for the pups. The water was shallow here and the current not too strong.

"Ruff! Ruff!" Encouraging barks came from Gran. She swam back, looking like a seal with her slick, shiny fur. She gave Grey's brother some help, pushing him on with her nose.

Suddenly, Grey saw a fish. It flashed beneath him, silver and glittering. He swiped at it with his paw. Missed! With excited yaps, he dived down into the water. Bubbles came back up – but Grey didn't. A strong current caught him and dragged him downstream. Grey bobbed to the surface, howling pitifully, his paws thrashing. But the river was raging, boiling with spray and foam. It swept the wolf cub along and flung him over a waterfall.

High on the rocks above stood Grey's family.
They stared down into the swirling pool at the
foot of the falls. There was no sign of the wolf cub.

The family made a circle, threw back their
heads and started to call for Grey. Their howls
rose above the waterfall's thunder and carried for
miles. Their howls meant, "We're up here! Come
to us!"

Grey didn't howl back. And he didn't return to
his family either.

Finally the wolves gave up. They didn't dare spend any more time waiting for Grey. They had the other cubs to protect. They went loping off through the forest, following the deer.

Every so often, as she ran though the trees, Grey's mum threw back her head and howled mournfully. There was no reply.

Where was her lost son? What had happened to him?

Chapter 4 – All alone

A long way downstream, the river threw
Grey onto a sandy bank. He lay soggy and
half-drowned, battered by the roaring water.
Once he could breathe freely again he licked
himself all over. Then he staggered to his feet
and looked around for his family. They were
nowhere in sight.

Frantically, Grey dashed up and down the
bank. For the first time in his life, he was on
his own. Suddenly the forest he had thought
was home felt like a very unfriendly place.

Grey whimpered in fear. His family made him feel safe and well defended. How could he survive without them?

"Owww! Owww!" He threw back his head and howled, long frightened cries that meant, "I'm here. Come and get me." But there were no answering howls from his family.

Grey snuffled the ground and smelled the air. He couldn't even pick up their scent. He shook himself, spray flying from his coat, and set off to find them.

By midday, with the sun burning high above him, the wolf cub was weary. He threw himself down, panting, in the shade of a bush. He whimpered with hunger, loneliness and fear. He dug with his muzzle in the dirt where a fat pink worm squirmed. Grey sucked it up, still wriggling, into his mouth.

Worms were tasty, but Grey was a growing wolf cub and he needed a proper meal. Hunger gnawed at his insides. He howled again. He wanted Mum to bring him meat. He wanted to play fight with his brothers and sisters. He wanted his family back to keep him safe from harm.

He picked up a piece of bark and chewed on it for comfort.

There! Suddenly, Grey's sharp eyes saw movement.

The grass stems shook. Grey pounced, quick as lightning, and found a rat under his front paws. He didn't even have to bite it, as Grandma had shown him. It died instantly of shock.

Grey swallowed the rat in only two gulps. Happier now, he set off to find his pack, sniffing and scent marking along the way.

Before long, he smelled wolf scent.

Through the trees, Grey saw a dark, slinking shape. Joyfully, he rushed towards it. His barks said, "It's me. I'm back!"

But when the wolf turned, Grey saw it was a stranger, a big she-wolf. She growled at him, a menacing growl that rumbled deep in her throat. Grey had strayed into another pack's territory.

Grey should have run for his life, but he didn't. Instead, he whined and whimpered and rolled over, hoping the she-wolf would feed and defend him, just like his own family did.

"Grrr!" The she-wolf sprang towards him, eyes blazing, fangs bared. It was hard enough feeding her own cubs, without another mouth to feed.

Grey scurried off, yelping. He ran until he thought he was safe and then he ran until he couldn't run any more. Finally he stopped, panting, his pink tongue lolling out. That was when the hunter shot him.

Chapter 5 – Stag attack!

Now Grey was injured, hiding in thorn bushes, licking his wound.

"I'm sure I hit him," thought the hunter, as he watched and waited. Still no sound came from the bushes. Grey stayed quiet, as he had been taught to do when danger was near.

An hour passed, maybe more.

"Maybe he died in there," the hunter thought. There was no way he could get the wolf's body out of that thorny tangle. Besides, it would soon be dark and he didn't want to be caught in the forest alone after night fall.

He sighed, "I'm having no luck at all today." He was going to have to do without that wolf skin.

He trudged off, through the forest.

Grey stayed in the thorn bushes for two days.
He licked dew from the ground and clawed in
the soil for grubs and beetles. When he finally
crawled out, his wound was healing, but he was
weak with thirst and hunger.

Again, he threw back his head and howled for
his family, "Owww! Owww!" He really needed
them now. With them he felt strong. Without
them he felt scared and defenceless.

Grey's howl echoed off the rocks. Then his ears pricked up. As the echoes died he was sure he heard answering howls. Grey's tail wagged excitedly. Was it his family? He listened again and then whined with disappointment. Grey could recognise each of his family's voices. This wasn't his family. It was some other wolf pack. This time Grey didn't run towards it. He'd learned his lesson: beware of strange wolves. They didn't welcome other wolves' lost cubs.

Grey crawled towards a muddy puddle and drank deeply. Through the trees, he saw light. He trotted out of the dark forest and found himself on a wide, sunny plain.

He sniffed the air. There was food out there! A herd of deer was grazing on the plain. Grey circled around it. He should have kept quiet and sneaked up, but hunger made him frantic and he dashed in, barking noisily. The deer saw him and bolted.

Grey was desperately hungry so, despite being small, he set off after the deer. Instinct told him to go for the little ones. But a big stag turned towards him and stood its ground. It lashed out with its hooves, defending the fawns. One blow from those hooves could crush a wolf's skull. The stag snorted, lowered its great antlers and charged.

Those antlers could have killed Grey, but he remembered the games with Gran. "*Antlers are sharp. They hurt. Watch out!*" Grey danced sideways out of the way and raced off, yelping – straight into a flock of crows.

Cawing, the big, black birds flapped
into the air. They had been feeding on the
remains of a wolf kill. Grey gorged himself on
what they had left. He teared off meat from
the deer carcass and crunched bones with his
teeth to get the marrow.

For the first time since he'd lost his family,
Grey slept that night with a full belly. But
could he look after himself in the days
to come?

Chapter 6 – Leader of the pack

A year later, a magnificent grey wolf padded though the wilderness. His eyes were bright, his coat glossy, his head held proudly. It was Grey, now fully-grown. A lot had happened since he'd been a starving, lost wolf cub. Somehow, against all the odds, he had survived. With what he had learned from his family and then found out for himself, he was now a skilled hunter. Now, he could defend himself if he had to.

But he still missed his family, their voices and scents. Now and again he howled for them. Other wolves sometimes called back, but not his family.

He howled now – long, eerie howls that echoed through the trees. Faint howls answered and Grey's whole body quivered with excitement. It wasn't his family, but those howls told him a story. The loudest, longest howls always come from the pack leader. Then the other wolves join in. In this pack though, there was no leader. No howls sounded above the rest saying, "I lead this pack! I'm big and fierce! Keep away!"

There could be many reasons why this pack had no leader. The leader could have been shot by a hunter killed by a blow from a stag's hoof. It could have died from old age.

Grey didn't think about reasons. This pack needed a new leader and Grey longed to be part of a pack again. He went trotting through the forest, following the howls.

After miles of running, Grey stopped to sniff the ground. He was on the edge of the pack's territory. Their howling was now very loud.

Grey was taking a big risk. Would the other pack accept him? Or would they attack him, as the she-wolf had done when he was a cub? Grey saw adult wolves, on a hill, watching him. He ran in barking, ready to defend himself with his strong, sharp teeth.

A wolf raced down the hill to challenge him. It sprang at Grey, barking furiously. Froth flew from its jaws. It tried to grab Grey by the throat, but Grey was quicker. He forced the other wolf to the ground. They wrestled, but Grey came out on top, pinning the other wolf to the ground with his front paws.

Grey barked, as if to say, "I won!"

His rival stopped struggling. Instead, it whined and licked Grey's muzzle. That meant, "I accept you as pack leader."

Then the other wolves came down and welcomed Grey, with friendly licks and sniffs. They danced around him, barking and wagging their tails. They had found their new leader. Grey wasn't a lone wolf any more.

That night, on the hilltop, Grey threw back his head and howled. He was telling all other packs, "I'm leader here now. Don't come near!"

But some wolves hadn't got the message.

41

Chapter 7 – Invaders!

The forest was a muddle of shadows and moonlight, but Grey could see them. They were sneaking up towards his hill, invading his territory, threatening his pack. Grey stopped howling. He became quiet and watchful, remembering Grandma's lessons from long ago.

Grey's new pack stood behind him, ready to defend each other. But the other pack was bigger and they had a strong leader. He'd spread his pack out, surrounding the hill. They were sneaking up silently through the bushes.

Grey's pack was trapped on the hilltop.
Grey didn't want to fight. Wolves always avoid
fighting, if they can. But he knew he might
not have a choice.

Suddenly, the other pack leader howled.
Grey lifted his head in surprise. A shiver went
through his body. It couldn't be, could it?

The howl came again. Grey picked up a
familiar scent. He whimpered, as if he was a
cub again. There was a rustling beside him and
suddenly he was staring into the glittering eyes
of a large wolf. It was his father.

They sniffed, touched noses, gave joyful barks.
Then the rest of Grey's family came rushing up:
his mum, his aunts and uncles, his sisters and
brothers now grown up, just like him.

Even Gran was still alive, leaner, more grizzled, but still keeping cubs in order. Behind her were two half-grown cubs from last year's litter.

Grey's family greeted their long-lost son. They leapt around him, yapping, tails wagging, in a happy reunion.

Grey barked at his own pack. His barks meant, "Don't be scared."

They came forward warily. Would they have to fight? Or would Grey's family be friendly? Only time would tell ...

Two years later, a little plane flew over the wilderness where the wolves lived.

"See that?" said the pilot, looking down. "Wild wolves! What a beautiful sight!"

A wolf pack in single file was running across the plains, off on a hunting mission.

"There must be fifty of them!" said his passenger. "I've never seen a pack that big!"

They didn't know that Grey's pack and his family hadn't fought each other. Instead they'd become friends. They'd joined forces, to make one mighty wolf pack. At first Grey's dad had run at its head. But when he became older and slower, he'd handed over leadership to Grey. Now Grey was head of the largest wolf pack in the forest. Together, they were strong. They played together, hunted together, raised cubs together. But most of all they defended each other.

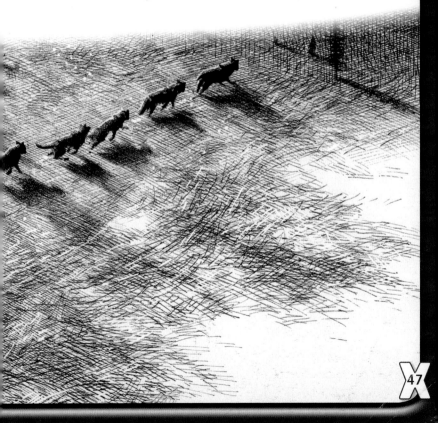

Wolves in the wild

- A wolf pack can have between two and twenty wolves in it. A male and female wolf will lead the pack. These are called the alpha male and female.

- Wolves howl to keep in touch with the rest of their pack. It means that they can talk to each other over great distances.

- Wolves have a thick coat of fur that helps them keep warm in winter. They have bristled hairs and blunt claws on their paws. These help them grip on slippery surfaces, like snow.

- In many parts of the world, wolves are listed as 'endangered'. This means that there are not many of them left.